Helen Steiner Rice

A Collection of Love Gifts

BARBOUR
PUBLISHING, INC.
Uhrichsville, Ohio

 *I*f you know the poems of Helen Steiner Rice, you know this book will bring you page after page of the soaring uplift, the inspiring faith, the spiritual challenge, and the down-to-earth directness that always speak to the heart.

If you haven't yet fallen in love with this amazing author, let us introduce her to you with a few comments based on her name:

H—Humility. "I am a very ordinary person," this woman whose writings have sold in the millions always insisted. But she had the extraordinary gift of bringing ordinary people life-changing inspiration, faith, and hope.

E—Empathy. Losing her husband almost as soon as she married, Helen Steiner Rice knew the depths of shadow—and the heights of sunshine—that can touch any soul. Readers immediately sense that she is attuned to every human emotion.

L—Love. These verses demonstrate her heartwarming love for her fellow humans, for God's beautiful creation, and for the Creator Himself.

E—Enthusiasm. The word means "God within." Helen was filled with His spirit of contagious interest in everyone and everything, a spirit of zest for life and vibrant creativity.

N—Naturalness. Many people don't read poetry because it seems to be written in an unknown tongue. The writings of Helen Steiner Rice are so readable because they are in words everyone can immediately appreciate.

S—Spiritual Strength. Thousands of readers draw divine power for living from these verses.

T—Thankfulness. The spirit of gratitude to God for His wonderful world and His love and grace overflows each word.

E—Energy. We sense a divine empowerment as Helen's lyrics fill our minds.

I—Inspiration. Although this word is much overworked today, men and women who feel they have hit bottom constantly find in these lines the inspiring courage to soar again.

N—Neighborliness. When you read one of these poems, you immediately feel in touch with a kindred spirit, a spiritual neighbor. Helen Steiner Rice's writings, published in many countries, make her Neighbor to the World.

E—Enlightenment. A little boy, used to seeing saints in stained glass windows, said, "A saint is somebody that lets the light through." These poems lighten our dark corners by helping us see the Light of the World.

R—Radiance. The radiant optimism and faith and love that characterized the author's life shine through her writings.

R—Religion. Although this word often has negative connotations today, the apostle James wrote, "Pure religion and undefiled before God and the Father is this, To visit the fatherless and widows in their affliction, and to keep himself unspotted from the world" (James 1:27). Helen Steiner Rice's life was filled with that kind of loving concern and dedication, and these writings reflect it.

I—Intelligence. Not the abstract intellectualism of the ivory-towered philosopher, but the practical, spiritual wisdom of the Bible shines through Helen's writings.

C—Comfort. Tragedy strikes us all, sooner or later. The inspiring thoughts in these verses have enabled thousands of readers to face the aftermath of disappointment and sorrow with the consolation of renewed courage and confidence.

E—Excellence. The Book of Proverbs ends with the words, "Many daughters have done virtuously, but thou excellest them all....Give her of the fruit of her hands, and let her own works praise her in the gates" (Proverbs 31:29-31). We believe the excellence of these works speaks for itself. "Let her own works praise her."

We are proud to present these Love Gifts from one of the world's best-loved authors, Helen Steiner Rice.

The Publisher

The Magic of Love

Love is like *magic* and it always will be,
    for love still remains *life's sweet mystery!*
Love works in ways that are wondrous and strange
    and there's *nothing in life* that *love*
    cannot change!
Love can transform the most commonplace
    into beauty and splendor and sweetness
    and grace!
Love is unselfish, understanding and kind,
    for it sees with its *heart* and not with its mind!
Love is the answer that everyone seeks—
Love is the language that every heart speaks—
Love can't be bought, it is priceless and free,
Love like pure *magic* is a *sweet mystery!*

Helen Steiner Rice

Warm Our Hearts with Thy Love

Oh, God, who made the summer
    and warmed the earth with beauty,
Warm our hearts with gratitude
    and devotion to our duty,
For in this age of violence,
    rebellion and defiance
We've forgotten the true meaning
    of "dependable reliance"—
We have lost our sense of duty
    and our sense of values, too,
And what was once unsanctioned,
    no longer is taboo,
Our standards have been lowered
    and we resist all discipline,
And our vision has been narrowed
    and blinded to all sin—

Oh, put the summer brightness
    in our closed, unseeing eyes
So in the careworn faces
    that we pass we'll recognize
The heartbreak and the loneliness,
    the trouble and despair
That a word of understanding
    would make easier to bear—
Oh, God, look down on our cold hearts
    and warm them with Your love,
And grant us Your forgiveness
    which we're so unworthy of.

Make Your Day Bright by Thinking Right

Don't start your day by supposin'
   that trouble is just ahead,
It's better to stop supposin'
   and start with a prayer instead,
And make it a prayer of *Thanksgiving*
   for the wonderful things God has wrought
Like the beautiful sunrise and sunset,
   "God's gifts" that are free
   and not bought—
For what is the use of supposin'
   the dire things that could happen to you
And worry about some misfortune
   that seldom if ever comes true—
But instead of just idle supposin'
   step forward to meet each new day

Secure in the knowledge God's near you
    to lead you each step of the way—
For supposin' the worst things will happen
    only helps to make them come true
And you darken the bright, happy moments
    that the dear Lord has given to you—
So if you desire to be happy
    and get rid of the *"misery of dread"*
Just give up *"supposin' the worst things"*
    and look for *"the best things"* instead.

A Favorite Recipe

Take a *cup* of *kindness*,
    mix it well with *love*,
Add a lot of Patience
    and *faith* in *God above*,
Sprinkle very generously
    with *joy* and *thanks* and *cheer*—
And you'll have lots of *"angel food"*
    to feast on all the year.

Things to Be Thankful For

The good, green earth beneath our feet,
The air we breathe, the food we eat,
Some work to do, a goal to win,
A hidden longing deep within
That spurs us on to bigger things
And helps us meet what each day brings,
All these things and many more
Are things we should be thankful for...
And most of all our thankful prayers
Should rise to God because He cares!

There's Sunshine in a Smile

Life is a mixture of sunshine and rain,
Laughter and pleasure, teardrops and pain,
All days can't be bright, but it's certainly true,
There was never a cloud
    the sun didn't shine through—
So just keep on smiling whatever betide you,
Secure in the knowledge
    God is always beside you,
And you'll find when you smile
    your day will be brighter
And all of your burdens
    will seem so much lighter—
For each time you smile you will find it is true
Somebody, somewhere will *smile back at you,*
And nothing on earth
    can make life more worthwhile
Than the sunshine and warmth
    of a *beautiful smile.*

Helen Steiner Rice

What More Can You Ask

God's love endureth forever—
What a wonderful thing to know
When the tides of life run against you
And your spirit is downcast and low...
God's kindness is ever around you,
Always ready to freely impart
Strength to your faltering spirit,
Cheer to your lonely heart...
God's presence is ever beside you,
As near as the reach of your hand,
You have but to tell Him your troubles,
There is nothing He won't understand...
And knowing God's love is unfailing,
And His mercy unending and great,
You have but to trust in His promise—
"God comes not too soon or too late"...
So wait with a heart that is patient
For the goodness of God to prevail—
For never do prayers go unanswered,
And His mercy and love never fail.

Never Borrow Sorrow from Tomorrow

Deal only with the present,
Never step into tomorrow,
For God asks us just to trust Him
And to never borrow sorrow—
For the future is not ours to know
And it may never be,
So let us live and give our best
And give it lavishly—
For to meet tomorrow's troubles
Before they are even ours
Is to anticipate the Saviour
And to doubt His all-wise powers—
So let us be content to solve
Our problems one by one,
Asking nothing of tomorrow
Except *"Thy will be done."*

If You Meet God in the Morning, He'll Go with You through the Day

"The earth is the Lord's
   and the fulness thereof"—
It speaks of His greatness,
   it sings of His love,
And each day at dawning
   I lift my heart high
And raise up my eyes
   to the infinite sky...
I watch the night vanish
   as a new day is born,
And I hear the birds sing
   on the wings of the morn,

I see the dew glisten
    in crystal-like splendor
While God, with a touch
    that is gentle and tender,
Wraps up the night
    and softly tucks it away
And hangs out the sun
    to herald a new day...
And so I give thanks
    and my heart kneels to pray—
"God, keep me and guide me
    and go with me today."

He Asks So Little and Gives So Much

What must I do
    to insure peace of mind?
Is the answer I'm seeking
    too hard to find?
How can I know
    what God wants me to be?
How can I tell
    what's expected of me?
Where can I go
    for guidance and aid
To help me correct
    the errors I've made?
The answer is found
    in doing *three things*

And great is the gladness
    that doing them brings...
"Do justice"—"Love kindness"—
    "Walk humbly with God"—
For with these *three things*
    as your "rule and your rod"
All things worth having
    are yours to achieve
If you follow God's words
    and have *faith to believe!*

The Power of Love

There is no thinking person
 who can stand untouched today
And view the world around us
 drifting downward to decay
Without feeling deep within them
 a silent unnamed dread,
Wondering how to stem the chaos
 that lies frightfully ahead...
But the problems we are facing
 cannot humanly be solved
For our diplomatic strategy
 only gets us more involved
And our skillful ingenuity,
 our technology and science
Can never change a sinful heart
 filled with hatred and defiance...

So our problems keep on growing
    every hour of every day
As man vainly tries to solve them
    in his own *self-willful way*...
But man is powerless alone
    to *clean up the world outside*
Until his own polluted soul
    is *clean and free inside*...
For the amazing power of love
    is beyond all comprehension
And it alone can heal this world
    of its hatred and dissension.

Someone Cares

Someone cares and always will,
The world forgets but God loves you still,
You cannot go beyond His Love
No matter what you're guilty of—
For God forgives until the end,
He is your faithful, loyal friend,
And though you try to hide your face
There is no shelter any place
That can escape His watchful eye,
For on the earth and in the sky
He's ever present and *always there*
To take you in His tender care
And bind the wounds and mend the breaks
When all the world around forsakes...
Someone cares and *loves you still*
And *God* is *the Someone* who always will.

Finding Faith in a Flower

Sometimes when faith is running low
And I cannot fathom *why things are so*...
I walk alone among the flowers I grow
And learn the *"answers"* to *all I would know!*
For among my flowers I have come to see
Life's *miracle* and its *mystery*...
And standing in silence and reverie
My *faith comes flooding back to me!*

Let Go and Let God!

When you're troubled and worried
    and sick at heart
And your plans are upset and your world
    falls apart,
Remember God's ready and waiting to share
The burden you find much too heavy to bear—
So with faith, *"let go"* and *"let God"* lead the way
Into a brighter and less troubled day.

The Peace of Meditation

So we may know God better
And feel His quiet power,
Let us daily keep in silence
A *meditation hour*—
For to understand God's greatness
And to use His gifts each day
The soul must learn to meet Him
In a meditative way,
For our Father tells His children
That if they would know His will
They must seek Him in the silence
When all is calm and still…
For nature's greatest forces
Are found in quiet things
Like softly falling snowflakes
Drifting down on angels' wings,
Or petals dropping soundlessly
From a lovely full-blown rose,

So God comes closest to us
When our souls are in repose...
So let us plan with prayerful care
To always allocate
A certain portion of each day
To be still and meditate...
For when everything is quiet
And we're lost in meditation,
Our soul is then preparing
For a deeper dedication
That will make it wholly possible
To quietly endure
The violent world around us—
For in God we are secure.

"Flowers Leave Their Fragrance on the Hand That Bestows Them"

There's an old Chinese proverb
    that, if practiced each day,
Would change the whole world
    in a wonderful way—
Its truth is so simple,
    it's so easy to do,
And it works every time
    and successfully, too...
For you can't do a kindness
    without a reward,

Not in silver nor gold
    but in joy from the Lord—
You can't light a candle
    to show others the way
Without feeling the warmth
    of that bright little ray...
And you can't pluck a rose,
    all fragrant with dew,
Without part of its fragrance
    remaining with you.

Open My Eyes

God open my eyes
    so I may see
And feel Your presence
    close to me...
Give me strength
    for my stumbling feet
As I battle the crowd
    on life's busy street,
And widen the vision
    of my unseeing eyes
So in passing faces
    I'll recognize
Not just a stranger,
    unloved and unknown,

But a friend with a heart
  that is much like my own...
Give me perception
  to make me aware
That scattered profusely
  on life's thoroughfare
Are the best *gifts* of *God*
  that we daily pass by
As we look at the world
  with an *unseeing eye.*

Thank You, God, for Everything

Thank You, God, for everything—
    the big things and the small,
For "every good gift comes from God"—
    the giver of them all—
And all too often we accept
    without any thanks or praise
The gifts God sends as blessings
    each day in many ways,
And so at this *Thanksgiving time*
    we offer up a prayer
To thank You, God, for giving us
    a lot more than our share...
First, thank You for the little things
    that often come our way,
The things we take for granted
    but don't mention when we pray,
The unexpected courtesy,
    the thoughtful, kindly deed,

A hand reached out to help us
in the time of sudden need...
Oh, make us more aware, dear God,
of little daily graces
That come to us with "sweet surprise"
from never-dreamed-of places—
Then, thank You for the *"Miracles"*
we are much too blind to see,
And give us new awareness
of our many gifts from Thee,
And help us to remember
that the *Key* to *Life* and *Living*
Is to make each prayer a *Prayer of Thanks*
and every day *Thanksgiving.*

Helen Steiner Rice

A Sure Way to a Happy Day

Happiness is something
    we create in our mind,
It's not something you search for
    and so seldom find—
It's just waking up
    and beginning the day
By counting our blessings
    and kneeling to pray—
It's giving up thoughts
    that breed discontent
And accepting what comes
    as a "gift heaven-sent"—
It's giving up wishing
    for things we have not

And making the best of
    whatever we've got—
It's knowing that life
    is determined for us,
And pursuing our tasks
    without fret, fume or fuss—
For it's by completing
    what God gives us to do
That we find real contentment
    and happiness, too.

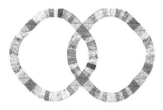

It's a Wonderful World

In spite of the fact
   we complain and lament
And view this old world
   with much discontent,
Deploring conditions
   and grumbling because
There's so much injustice
   and so many flaws,
It's a wonderful world
   and it's people like you
Who make it that way
   by the things that they do—
For a warm, ready smile
   or a kind, thoughtful deed,
Or a hand outstretched
   in an hour of need

Can change our whole outlook
    and make the world bright
Where a minute before
    just nothing seemed right—
It's a *wonderful world*
    and it always will be
If we keep our eyes open
    and focused to see
The *wonderful things*
    man is capable of
When he opens his heart
    to *God* and *His love*.

Helen Steiner Rice

He Loves You!

It's amazing and incredible,
But it's as true as it can be,
God loves and understands us all
And that means *you* and *me*—
His grace is all sufficient
For both the *young* and *old*,
For the lonely and the timid,
For the brash and for the bold—
His love knows no exceptions,
So never feel excluded
No matter *who* or *what* you are
Your name has been included—
And no matter what your past has been,
Trust God to understand,
And no matter what your problem is
Just place it in His Hand—
For in all of our *unloveliness*
This *great God loves us still,*
He loved us since the world began
And what's more, *He always will!*

Good Morning, God!

You are ushering in another day
Untouched and freshly new
So here I come to ask You, God,
If You'll renew me, too,
Forgive the many errors
That I made yesterday
And let me try again, dear God,
To walk closer in *Thy way...*
But, Father, I am well aware
I can't make it on my own
So *take my hand* and *hold it tight*
For I can't *walk alone!*

Helen Steiner Rice

Look on the Sunny Side

There are always two sides,
    the *good* and the *bad*,
The *dark* and the *light*,
    the *sad* and the *glad*—
But in looking back over
    the *good* and the *bad*
We're aware of the number
    of *good things* we've had—
And in counting our blessings
    we find when we're through
We've no reason at all
    to complain or be blue—
So thank God for *good* things
    He has already done,
And be grateful to Him
    for the battles you've won,
And know that the same God
    who helped you before

Is ready and willing
     to help you once more—
Then with faith in your heart
     reach out for God's Hand
And accept what He sends,
     though you can't understand—
For *Our Father* in heaven
     always knows what is best,
And if you trust in His wisdom
     your life will be blest,
For always remember
     that whatever betide you,
You are never alone
     for God is beside you.

Count Your Gains and Not Your Losses

As we travel down life's busy road
    complaining of our heavy load,
We often think God's been unfair
    and gave us much more than our share
Of little daily irritations
    and disappointing tribulations...
We're discontented with our lot
    and all the "bad breaks" that we got,
We count our losses, not our gain,
    and remember only tears and pain...
The good things we forget completely
    when God looked down and blessed us
    sweetly,
Our troubles fill our every thought,
    we dwell upon lost goals we sought,
And wrapped up in our own despair
    we have no time to see or share

Another's load that far outweighs
    our little problems and dismays...
And so we walk with head held low
    and little do we guess or know
That someone near us on life's street
    is burdened deeply with defeat...
But if we'd but forget *our care*
    and stop in sympathy to share
The burden that "our brother" carried,
    our mind and heart would be less harried
And we would feel our load was small,
    in fact, *we carried no load at all.*

Helen Steiner Rice

Fathers Are Wonderful People

Fathers are wonderful people
    too little understood,
And we do not sing their praises
    as often as we should...
For, somehow, Father seems to be
    the man who pays the bills,
While Mother binds up little hurts
    and nurses all our ills...
And Father struggles daily
    to live up to *"his image"*
As protector and provider
    and "hero of the scrimmage"...
And perhaps that is the reason
    we sometimes get the notion
That Fathers are not subject
    to the thing we call emotion,

But if you look inside Dad's heart,
    where no one else can see,
You'll find he's sentimental
    and as "soft" as he can be…
But he's so busy every day
    in the grueling race of life,
He leaves the sentimental stuff
    to his partner and his wife…
But Fathers are just *wonderful*
    in a million different ways,
And they merit loving compliments
    and accolades of praise,
For the only reason Dad aspires
    to fortune and success
Is to make the family proud of him
    and to bring them happiness…
And like *Our Heavenly Father,*
    he's a guardian and a guide,
Someone that we can count on
    to be *always on our side.*

Daily Prayers Dissolve Your Cares

I meet God in the morning
And go with Him through the day,
Then in the stillness of the night
Before sleep comes I pray
That God will just "take over"
All the problems I couldn't solve
And in the peacefulness of sleep
My cares will all dissolve,
So when I open up my eyes
To greet another day
I'll find myself renewed in strength
And there'll open up a way
To meet what seemed impossible
For me to solve alone
And once again I'll be assured
I am never *"on my own"*...
For if we try to stand alone

We are weak and we will fall,
For God is always *Greatest*
When we're helpless, lost and small,
And no day is unmeetable
If on rising our first thought
Is to thank God for the blessings
That His loving care has brought…
For there can be no failures
Or hopeless, unsaved sinners
If we enlist the help of God
Who makes all losers winners…
So meet Him in the morning
And go with Him through the day
And thank Him for His guidance
Each evening when you pray,
And if you follow faithfully
This daily way to pray
You will never in your lifetime
Face another "hopeless day."

My Garden of Prayer

My garden beautifies my yard
    and adds fragrance to the air...
But it is also *my cathedral*
    and *my quiet place of prayer*...
So little do we realize
    that *"the glory* and *the power"*
Of He who made the *universe*
    lies hidden in a flower.

Thank God for Little Things

Thank You, God, for little things
    that often come our way—
The things we take for granted
    but don't mention when we pray—
The unexpected courtesy,
    the thoughtful, kindly deed—
A hand reached out to help us
    in the time of sudden need—
Oh make us more aware, dear God,
    of little daily graces
That come to us with "sweet surprise"
    from never-dreamed-of places.

Helen Steiner Rice

Brighten the Corner Where You Are

We cannot all be famous
    or be listed in *"Who's Who,"*
But every person great or small
    has important work to do,
For seldom do we realize
    the importance of small deeds
Or to what degree of greatness
    unnoticed kindness leads—
For it's not the big celebrity
    in a world of fame and praise,
But it's doing unpretentiously
    in undistinguished ways
The work that God assigned to us,
    unimportant as it seems,
That makes our task outstanding
    and brings reality to dreams—
So do not sit and idly wish
    for wider, new dimensions

Where you can put in practice
    your many *"good intentions"*—
But at the spot God placed you
    begin at once to do
Little things to brighten up
    the lives surrounding you,
For if everybody brightened up
    the spot on which they're standing
By being more considerate
    and a little less demanding,
This dark old world would very soon
    eclipse the "Evening Star"
If everybody *brightened up*
    the corner where they are!

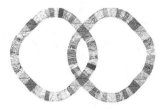

Helen Steiner Rice

It Takes the Bitter and the Sweet to Make a Life Full and Complete

Life is a mixture
      of sunshine and rain,
Laughter and teardrops,
      pleasure and pain—
Low tides and high tides,
      mountains and plains,
Triumphs, defeats
      and losses and gains—
But *always* in *all ways*
      God's guiding and leading

And He alone knows
  the things we're most needing—
And when He sends sorrow
  or some dreaded affliction,
Be assured that it comes
  with God's kind benediction—
And if we accept it
  as a *gift of His love,*
We'll be showered with blessings
  from *Our Father above.*

Helen Steiner Rice

"On the Wings of Prayer"

Just close your eyes
    and open your heart
And feel your worries
    and cares depart,
Just yield yourself
    to the Father above
And let Him hold you
    secure in His love—
For life on earth
    grows more involved
With endless problems
    that can't be solved—
But God only asks us
    to do our best,
Then He will "take over"
    and finish the rest—
So when you are tired,
    discouraged and blue,

There's always one door
    that is open to you—
And that is the door
    to "The House of Prayer"
And you'll find God waiting
    to meet you there,
And "The House of Prayer"
    is no farther away
Than the quiet spot
    where you kneel and pray—
For the heart is a temple
    when God is there
As we place ourselves
    in His loving care,
And He hears every prayer
    and answers each one
When we pray in His name
    "Thy will be done"—
And the burdens that seemed
    too heavy to bear
Are lifted away
    on *"the wings of prayer."*

Great Faith That Smiles Is Born of Great Trials

It's easy to say *"In God we trust"*
When life is radiant and fair,
But the test of faith is only found
When there are burdens to bear—
For our claim to faith in the "sunshine"
Is really *no faith at all,*
For when roads are smooth and days are bright
Our need for God is so small,
And no one discovers the fullness
Or the greatness of God's love
Unless they have walked in the "darkness"
With only a *light* from *above*—

For the faith to endure whatever comes
Is born of sorrow and trials,
And strengthened only by discipline
And nurtured by self-denials—
So be not disheartened by troubles,
For trials are the "building blocks"
On which to erect a *fortress* of *faith*
Secure on God's "ageless rocks."

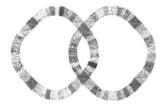

Helen Steiner Rice

When Troubles Assail You, God Will Not Fail You

When life seems empty
And there's no place to go,
When your heart is troubled
And your spirits are low,
When friends seem few
And nobody cares
There is always God
To hear your prayers—
And whatever you're facing
Will seem much less
When you go to God
And confide and confess,
For the burden that seems
Too heavy to bear
God lifts away
On the wings of prayer—

And seen through God's eyes
Earthly troubles diminish
And we're given new strength
To face and to finish
Life's daily tasks
As they come along
If we pray for strength
To keep us strong—
So go to Our Father
When troubles assail you
For His grace is sufficient
And He'll never fail you.

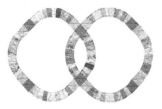

Helen Steiner Rice

Anywhere Is a Place of Prayer If God Is There

I have prayed on my knees in the morning,
I have prayed as I walked along,
I have prayed in the silence and darkness
And I've prayed to the tune of a song—
I have prayed in the midst of triumph
And I've prayed when I suffered defeat,
I have prayed on the sands of the seashore
Where the waves of the ocean beat—
I have prayed in a velvet-hushed forest
Where the quietness calmed my fears,
I have prayed through suffering and heartache
When my eyes were blinded with tears—
I have prayed in churches and chapels,
Cathedrals and synagogues, too,
But often I've had the feeling
That my prayers were not getting through,

And I realized then that Our Father
Is not really concerned where we pray
Or impressed by our manner of worship
Or the eloquent words that we say…
He is only concerned with our feelings,
And He looks deep into our heart
And hears the "cry of our soul's deep need"
That no words could ever impart…
So it isn't the prayer that's expressive
Or offered in some special spot,
It's the sincere plea of a sinner
And God can tell whether or not
We honestly seek His forgiveness
And earnestly mean what we say,
And then and then only He answers
The prayer that we fervently pray.

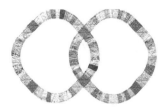

How Great the Yield from a Fertile Field

The farmer ploughs through the fields of green
And the blade of the plough is sharp and keen,
But the seed must be sown to bring forth grain,
For nothing is born without suffering
    and pain—
And God never ploughs in the soul of man
Without intention and purpose and plan,
So whenever you feel the plough's sharp blade
Let not your heart be sorely afraid
For, like the farmer, God chooses a field
From which He expects an excellent yield—
So rejoice though your heart is broken in two,
God seeks to bring forth a rich harvest in you.

Help Yourself to Happiness

Everybody, everywhere
    seeks happiness, it's true,
But finding it and keeping it
    seems difficult to do,
Difficult because we think
    that happiness is found
Only in the places where
    wealth and fame abound—
And so we go on searching
    in "palaces of pleasure"
Seeking recognition
    and monetary treasure,
Unaware that happiness
    is just a "state of mind"
Within the reach of everyone
    who takes time to be kind—
For in making *others happy*
    we will be happy, too,
For the happiness you give away
    returns to "shine on you."

Give Lavishly!
Live Abundantly!

The more you give, the more you get—
The more you laugh, the less you fret—
The more you do *unselfishly*,
The more you live *abundantly*...

The more of everything you share,
The more you'll always have to spare—
The more you love, the more you'll find
That life is good and friends are kind...

For only *what we give away*,
Enriches us from day to day.